Transition from the Borrower to the Lender

Lessons to Change Your Financial Status

Lequita Gray

© 2014 Lequita Gray. All Rights Reserved.

No part of this publication may be reproduced or transmitted in any form or by any means, mechanical or electronic, including photocopying and recording, or by any information storage and retrieval system, without permission in writing from author or publisher (except by a reviewer, who may quote brief passages and/or show brief video clips in a review).

Legal information and disclaimer: The advice and strategies contained herein may not be suitable for your situation. You should consult with a professional where appropriate. The purchaser/reader of this publication assumes full responsibility for the use of these materials and information. Please consult applicable laws and regulations and competent counsel to ensure your use of this material conforms with applicable laws and regulations. Neither the publisher nor author shall be liable for any loss be it personal or commercial damages, including but not limited to special, incidental, consequential, or other damages.

Introduction

Hi there! I would like to take this opportunity to congratulate you on taking the first step in the transitioning process which was purchasing this book. In the pages to come you will find lessons that I have found successful in managing money for low income individuals. You will discover that while the amount of income you have plays a role in the type of lifestyle you have, what you do with the income plays a greater role. We will explore the role of the lender and the role of the borrower. You will see why it is better to be the lender. You will learn foundational principles to money management that will start you down the path of becoming a lender. Sounds good? Great! Let's get started.

1

Which Am I?

At some point or another along life's journey we will play both roles of the lender and the borrower. It is the way this society at this time and space works. For a moment think about what is a lender and what is a borrower in your mind. Who are they? A simple answer could be banks are lenders and people borrow money from banks. Other answers could be pawn shops or mortgage companies as lenders. Maybe it's mom and dad who are the lenders. All of these are great examples of lenders.

My definition of lender is an individual who uses his money to make more money through borrowers. The lender loans banks, corporations, and government money in the form of savings accounts, money market accounts, certificate deposits (CDs), stocks, and bonds. The lender acquires appreciable assets. The lender knows how to manage money. My definition of a borrower is an individual who borrows money at a premium to purchase things that he wants or needs. Looking at those two definitions, which person would you rather be?

There is nothing wrong with being a borrower. There is a problem when we live in the perpetual state of a borrower. There is a difference. When we live in the perpetual state of borrowing, we are not making any moves towards long term wealth. We do not consider future needs or future generations. We WORK for every dollar that comes through our hands. We do not show constraint in spending. We buy whatever we want despite not having actual cash to pay for it. We are stuck on the financial hamster wheel year after year going nowhere because we don't know how to become a lender. Why? It's because we think the bank is the lender. We think Freddie Mac, Fannie Mae, and Sally Mae are institutions. The truth is the bank is actually made up of many people who choose to be lenders. Freddie Mac, Fannie Mae, and Sally Mae use lenders' money to loan it to us. They are all middle men for ordinary people just like you and me who decide not to WORK for every dollar but instead make that dollar work for more dollars.

Now you may be thinking "It looks like I am a perpetual borrower." Deep breath. Sigh. Well, me too! That was me! Even now I am that person at times. I don't want to be so discipline. I don't want to follow a budget. Sometimes I just want be footloose and fancy-free. So don't feel down or depressed about being a borrower now. That's why you bought this book. You are on your way to becoming a lender.

2

Why Do You Money The Way You Do?

One day while working I pondered as to how was it possible for individuals who received less than $700 a month were able to lead fulfilling lives on that income? How were they able to build cushions in their bank accounts on such limited funds? There were a number of elements that contributed to their overall financial success. One of which was the role emotions had on spending habits. Emotions play a critical part in financial management. For a great deal of us humans, there are emotions tied to our money. These emotions can be triggered by any number of things associated with the experiences and lessons that have brought us to our current place in life. Businesses and marketing firms have made billions of dollars playing on emotional triggers. Stores place small impulse buys at the cash registers anticipating that the shoppers who are waiting will pick up a few more items that they do not need but want. This is the store's attempt to benefit from your emotions.

When attempting to set goals to get your finances in order and become a lender it is imperative to deal with the things that are going on inside your head. What is the underlying reason to the way you manage money? For some it is as simple as they were never taught the principles of money. I can remember learning how to fill out a check in school but the concept of managing the funds associated with the check was not included in the lesson. By the time I learned how to manage money I had already made a mess of my finances. Which category applies to you? Did you grow up poor and now that you have a steady income you overspend? Did you grow up in plenty and you overspend because you have always had what you wanted? Do you attempt to keep up with the Joneses? Do you associate your self-worth with designer clothes and fancy cars? Do you try to overcompensate to make up for what you feel are shortfalls in your life? Do you try to pay for love and affection? If the answer to any of these questions is yes then you are on the road to discovering the cause of your spending habits. Perhaps there is another reason that is not listed here. The reality is it does not matter how much money you have or earn, a poor emotional state will wreak havoc on your financial stability. It does not matter if you grew up poor. It is time to move past that. Look at the bright side you learned how to make it with what was available. Those days are behind you but they can also be ahead if you are not careful. The Joneses are not thinking about you so why are you trying to keep up with them? Someone will always have things whether it's a new car, a new house, a new bicycle or the latest electronics or their children have the latest electronics that you think you want. You tell yourself 'my children deserve those things'. What can you do? Are you putting yourself in financial distress trying to keep up appearances you can't afford and on the inside, when you get home away from the Joneses, you are depressed because you have created a mountain of bills that you do not have the ability to pay? Forget the Joneses! Don't follow the trend. Set the trend. When you find yourself comparing what you have to what others have, think about whether those things are necessary to live a fulfilling life. There is a time to take care of needs and there is a time to take care of wants. Things you need will certainly come before the things you want. The Joneses are maybe one paycheck away from bankruptcy themselves. Be happy for others' success but do not measure your value by what others have.

Why does having designer things make you feel good about yourself? Designer things are nice to have, however you need feel good about yourself with only the name your parents gave you. If this is an area where you struggle I want you to look in the mirror every day and say 'I love me.' Say 'I am wonderful.' Tell yourself 'I am great.' Affirm yourself at all times and it will not matter whose name you have on your back. You were given a name. Walk proud with it. The same thing is true for overcompensating for what you feel are shortfalls. Success requires failure. There cannot be one without the other. It is only through failure that you learn to be successful. This is true in life and business. Grow from your experiences and hold your head up high. Once you feel secure with who you are you position yourself to make decisions that are not based on unhealthy emotions.

What happens after the unhealthy emotional habits get under control? Great question! Individuals who successfully separate their emotions from their money are able to build and create wealth. You will actually begin to think about purchases as either a want or a need. Those things that are wants can be rationalized. Consider the effect the purchase will have on your bank account and your future plans. You will be able to recognize the behavior pattern and redirect yourself. Ultimately, being aware of you emotional triggers will help you to be more disciplined when managing your money.

Lenders are emotionally intelligent about their money.

3

Oh No, It's the Six Letter Word! Budget

Oh yes, it is the six letter word. Brace yourself for it. Budget, there I said it. Whether you know what it is or not, the truth is you have to fall in love with this word and its concept. Remember, lenders know how to manage money. What is a budget? A budget is an outline of your expenses and your income. You have to have a budget. Why? You need to know where your money is going or where your money needs to go. Have you ever had the experience where you get paid and three days later you wonder where the money went? You discover that you have more bills than money. You realize that a bill payment is due and you happened to have forgotten about that bill although you have been paying it for years. The mind becomes a tricky playground sometimes. Stress, pressure or just everyday life can make you forget about the most routine things. Having a budget will allow you to track your expenses without having to rely solely on your memory.

How do I devise a budget? That is a great question. It does not have to be fancy. All you need is a pen and a piece of paper. You can also use a computer. For the sake of simplicity, list every person or place you owe money. To the right of the name of the bill write how much the bill is monthly. Next to the amount of the bill write down the day of the month the bill is due. Your sheet should look similar to example 1.

Example 1

Bill	Amount	Due Date
Rent	$750	1st
Utilities	$200	15th
Car Note	$400	23rd
Groceries	$125	3rd
Supplies	$60	3rd
Gas	$120	
Credit Card 1	$25	10th
Credit Card 2	$15	17th

When creating a budget it is imperative to list ALL expenses necessary to live. In the example supplies are listed. Supplies are things such as household supplies and personal supplies. Some people choose not to include gas and groceries in the monthly budget. This is a terrible mistake. If you do not use gas, list the cost of transportation expenses.

Now that all the expenses are listed a payment schedule can be created. The payment schedule will coincide with your pay days. To begin, sort the expenses according to the due dates. Next, determine which items will be paid from the first paycheck of the month and which items will be paid from the second paycheck of the month. Some expenses, such as gas, may be funded from both paychecks. At the bottom of each column add all the expenses for the pay period. Below the total place the total amount of take home income below total for the corresponding pay day. Please only include income from work. Exclude income from alimony, child support, or any other source in which you do not work to receive at this time. *(The only exception is for those who receive income from Social Security. This income should be included in the budget.)*

Example 2 shows a simple format.

Example 2

Bill	**Pay Day 1**	**Pay Day 2**
Rent	$750	
Groceries	$125	
Supplies	$60	
Credit Card 1		$25
Gas	$60	$60
Utilities		$200
Car Note		$400
Insurance	$80	
Credit Card 2		$15
Total	$1075	$700
Total Income	$1100	$1100
Over +/Short -	+ $25	+ $400

Which pay period an expense is paid will change for those who are paid on a bi-weekly basis. Those who are paid once or twice a month will have the type of budget that when the expenses are paid will not change often. Regardless of how often the pay day comes, the budget will need to be reviewed and updated every month. Payments from others in the form of alimony and child support are not included in the budget. These items can be listed as income below the total income but they are not to be included in the income that is allotted to pay your monthly expenses. These items are intentionally excluded because I do not want you to become dependent on them to pay your monthly expenses. Instead, those sources of income are to be considered as butter on your bread. It tastes good, but it is not necessary. It's extra cash flow. If it comes that's great. If it doesn't come in there is not an impact on your ability to pay monthly expenses.

Alright, stand up and give yourself a round of applause. You just took another step towards financial stability and becoming a lender. You are awesome! Your budget, no matter how good or bad it looks, is a major asset to your financial future. Maybe you are surprised at what you discovered when you wrote everything out. Perhaps you discovered you are wasting a ton of money and you do not know where it is going. On the other hand, you may have discovered that you have more expenses than income. Regardless of the scenario, the next chapters will help with overcoming these barriers. The last thing to remember from this chapter is no matter how much income you have or money you have in the bank you always will need to maintain a budget.

Lender's manage their money and do not let their money manage them.

My Budget

Bill	Pay Day 1	Pay Day 2
Total		
Total Income		
Over +/Short -		

4

Making the Ends Meet

Trim Expenses

Now, you completed the budget and it looks like you have more going out than coming in. Perhaps you have a little more coming in than going out. Just maybe you have more than enough coming in than going out on paper but not in reality. For those of you who related to the first two statements I going to help you get to the place of those who related to the third statement (*but not quite*). Let me forewarn you. **This next step is going to take discipline, practice, and dedication.** There will be times when it is not fun. You will want to revert back to the old way. That is just human nature. If you hang in there and apply the principles there will be a great reward in your financial future.

There are times along life's journey that expenses exceed income. There are also times when you are trying to reach a life milestone like purchasing a house, buying a car, or saving for a vacation. When these occasions arise there is the question of how to do everything within the margins of your income. There are solutions for each scenario. When the expenses exceed the income it's time to remove expenses from the budget. The items that remain on the budget are those things that are necessary to LIVE. These things include food, shelter, and utilities. Next list the bills that must be paid or else such as student loans, Internal Revenue Service, child care, car payments, and insurance. Leave a space for savings on the budget after the necessary expenses. Now list the credit card bills and medical bills if you have any. Last list the luxury items that have a monthly expense such as cable, movie rentals, beauty regimes, and gym memberships. Now some of you may be saying to yourself, "I have to have my hair and nails done. I need my tanning services. I need my gym membership so I can look good." I have a response. My response is not right now. Please, don't put the book down. We will work out a compromise. Let's look at example 3.

Example 3

Rent	$700
Utilities	$250
Groceries	$300
Child Care	$476
Car Payment	$199
Gas	$200
Insurance	$65
Student Loans	$105
Savings	$5
Credit Card 1	$50
Credit Card 2	$25
Cable	$110
Cell Phone	$100
Home Phone	$50
Internet	$50
Gym Membership	$25
Dry Cleaning	$125
Total Expenses	**$2885**

Total Income $2400

The complete list should include everything that is paid out every month just like the budget. The first things to remove from the monthly budget are the things that you can do for yourself. If you can cook, clean, or do laundry then the maid, the restaurants, and the cleaners are the first to go off your list. The second group of expenses to remove is luxury items. Keep removing things from the budget until the expenses are less than the income.

What happens when there is nothing else that can be removed? It is at that point that you look for ways to reduce expenses. Call around and ask for a cheaper package. This may mean going to another cellular phone, internet, cable, or child care provider. You may need to move to more affordable housing. Here is a list of ways to save money.

- Pack your lunch- it is cheaper to take your lunch than buy it every day.
- Reduce/ditch cable package- this is a luxury item. If you do not watch much television you are wasting money paying for cable. Also, there are ways to stream your favorite shows with smart televisions or boxes that you can pay for

once. It is one of the best ways to open up money in your budget.
- Lose the landline phone- most people do not use this line if they have a cell phone. If you don't need it you can lose it.
- Switch to a cheaper internet package- pay for the amount of data you need. You can always increase the speed once your finances can stand it.
- Carpool to work- save money and the planet by carpooling to work.
- Wash your clothes instead of dry cleaning- this is a tricky one. This will only be successful if your wardrobe is not dry clean only. Otherwise you will end up needing to buy a new wardrobe.
- Do your own yard work- it's good exercise for the body and your wallet.
- Drink tap water- bottled water's mark-up is outrageous. If the tap water in your area is not the best, invest in a water filtration device.
- Buy generics and store brands- generic medication must meet the same guidelines as the brand name stuff. Store brand foods and products are often times as good and effective as the leading brand.

- Shop at discount grocery stores. You know the ones where you put a quarter in the basket and pay for bags. That's a cheap place to get fruit and other staples.
- Use coupons- only for the stuff you already intend to purchase. Using coupons for things you did not plan to buy does not save you any money.
- Lose the pay card and get a bank account- Pay cards often have higher fees than having a bank account. Stop paying a company for accessing your own money.
- Lower your cellular phone bill- only pay for what you use.
- Brew your own coffee- it's less expensive to make your coffee at home than picking it up from a drive-thru.
- Paint your own nails- you can still be cute and you can change your polish more often. (See I told you I had a compromise.)
- Do/Wear your own hair- if you have the ability to do your own hair, do it! If not, enlist a friend to do it for you. (Compromise again.)
- Stay away from the vending machine- that change on chips adds up.

- Pay your bills on time- avoid late fees whenever possible.
- Change your light bulbs to energy efficient bulbs- you can control your utility expense by turning off lights, adjusting the thermostat, and changing the light bulbs.
- Grow a small garden- it's healthy for you and your pocket book.
- Have a yard sale-go through your home and get rid of the extra stuff. Use the proceeds to pay off a bill.
- Exercise outside or at home- It's free. There are local parks with walking trails. Use them.

Sell your time and talents

Everyone is gifted with a talent. If you have not discovered it yet, keep looking. It's there. There are times when you have to supplement your income. If you can cook, sew, decorate, organize, paint, work on computers, draw, sculpt, play an instrument, or whatever else, do it for money. *Be sure to follow all IRS applicable laws for reporting income. I don't want you on the news because Uncle Sam wants his money.* Besides selling your skills to others, you can pick up another job if it will not impose on other obligations. Regardless of which method chosen to make more money, use the extra income to pay off debt. This prescription is not intended to be a permanent fix for a lifestyle that you ultimately cannot afford.

Lender's always look for ways to save money.

I will save money by:

5

Manage Your Credit

What is credit?

When I consider one of the decisions that has affected my financial stability and ability to attain wealth the most, it was deciding to get credit cards. Everything that I ever heard about credit cards was related to the benefit having them. I have to give the credit card companies recognition where it is due. They have very successful marketing campaigns. I can remember being a freshman in college. If you have attended college you know that those years can be the poorest times of your life. The maturity level of a college student is not where it needs to be even if you were taught about finances. I can still hear the man at the credit card booth on campus saying "Two free gifts for student today." He had a distinct accent that still rings clear. This was my first introduction to credit cards. It was wonderful. I got free gifts and a credit card to go buy something for the next fraternity or sorority party. Soon the wonder would turn into a nightmare because I did not have a job to pay the credit card bills. So what did I do? You guessed it! I took out another credit card to pay the previous one. Eventually, I had to get a job on campus to support my credit card expenses. Luckily today there are rules preventing such things on college campuses. I was living like a borrower. I was enjoying the satisfaction of being able to buy things and then living with regret when the bill came 25 days later. Living in the perpetual state of borrowing is cyclical. There are so many ups and downs. Some people never break out and live through this cycle year after year. I was lucky enough to wake up and with this book you will too. After ruining my credit in college, I paid all of that debt off, when I could, and restored a healthy credit score.

Simply stated, credit is a means of which to pay for things without money. It is a loan from a company that charges interest for borrowing. Throughout life there are times when having "good" credit is more important than others like when trying to purchase a home, buy a new car, or get a small business loan. Companies that you borrow money from send a report that is used by other lenders to tell them whether or not you are a good customer. The credit reporting agencies assigns a score based on your payment history. Credit scores range from 300 to 850. What affects your credit score? The way you pay your creditors, how much you owe as it relates to your available balance, consolidation, and bankruptcy are all things that affect your score. The focus of this book is to tell you how to become financially stable. As the program is implemented your credit score should gradually improve.

Credit cards do have a place in your wallet. I recommend ONE and only ONE credit card in your wallet. The purpose of this card is to make your life simpler when you go to pay for things such as rental cars, hotel rooms, and online purchases. Under absolutely no circumstances are you to finance rental cars, hotel rooms, and your online purchases. You are to pay for these services with the card and immediately pay the entire balance before the interest accrues.

When you have multiple credit cards with balances you are robbing yourself of wealth. How? You are paying credit card companies much more interest a month than they can earn through other investments. You are blindly contributing to the wealth of others instead of the wealth of yourself. Consider how many hours you have to work to even pay the credit card bill. Instead you can invest that money and get interest from other people who have not read this book and make more money. It is for this reason that I want you to forget about the Joneses. The Joneses are consumers. Consumers live the lifestyle of the perpetual borrower and they are rarely investors. Consumers give their money away. Investors lend their money to make more money. Remember, you are going to set the trend.

So what now? As you look at your budget, you see all types of creditor listed. It's okay.

You are about to pay each and every one of them off. There are many suggestions out there as to who to pay off first. The truth of the matter is all of them work if you put the program into action. Action takes discipline so you will have to exercise self-control for this advice to work. I want you to give priority to the accounts that are open. The accounts that are open have the most impact on your credit score right now. These are the accounts that are used to see how much of your available credit is being used. The higher percentage of available credit used will make your credit score fall. As the percentage lowers, your credit score rises. There are other factors that affect the score however, this is all the information needed for this exercise.

Look at your open accounts and select the one that will be the easiest to payoff. You are to pay this card off first. Look at your budget to determine how much extra you can put towards paying that account off. Next, I want you to look at the box on the credit card statement for each of your remaining credit cards that show how much is required monthly to pay the account in full in three years. Put the rest of your credit card bills on this schedule. In most cases it is not much more than the minimum payment.

Special Note: *The amount in the box will change as the balance decreases. This does not mean that you change it on your budget. That will start the three year clock over again.*

If the box is not located on your statement, call the company and ask them to calculate it for you. There are also calculators online and apps for your phone that can help.

If you have other creditors such as payday loans, doctor bills, and other loans include them in your payoff plan. Doctor's offices often request the full amount due. In my experience, they are willing to accept payments. For clarity sake, all creditors should be paid during this process.

When you pay one creditor off, use the excess funds to pay the next creditor off until all the balances are zero. Do not at any time close any open credit cards during this process. This will have an adverse effect on your credit score. After you have paid off all of your cards, it is your choice as to whether or not they remain open. Remember, my recommendation is for ONE card only. Leaving the other cards open will only lead to the temptation of spending unnecessarily. Once all of the open accounts' balances are paid, use the excess funds to pay off the closed accounts. At the end of the process, all open and closed accounts will be paid in full.

I once heard a man say messing up his credit was the best thing that happened to him. Why, because he now had to pay cash for everything and the good thing was he didn't have to worry about paying for it later. The purpose of losing the credit cards is to help you live within your means and to start to accumulate wealth. You can't become wealthy when you are enslaved to credit card debt.

Protect Your Name

Once you get on track to accomplishing your financial stability goals, people will approach you asking for things. Most of the time it is to borrow a few dollars here or there. There are times when people will ask for your name. What I mean by that is people will ask you to sign your name on things that they cannot get on their own. Examples of this are cars and loans. Remember in chapter two when I said you have a name be proud of it? The same holds true here. Your name is very precious. Protect it. Family and friends are very near and dear to just about everyone. We all want to look out for their best interest. There is nothing wrong with that. However, there are times to proceed with caution. When you are faced with someone asking you to sign your name to help them get a car or loan ask yourself a few questions.

1. Why does my loved one need me to co-sign for them?

If the answer is the person made a mess of their credit you should not co-sign for them. Buy them a copy of this book instead.

2. Can I make the payment if the person cannot?

When you co-sign for a loan you are saying that you will make the payment if the person you signed for cannot. If when you look at your budget you cannot afford to make the payment, you should not co-sign for the loan.

3. How many loans am I currently responsible for?

You want to limit how many outstanding loans you have for your household. This is especially true for automobile loans. I recommend one and only one car loan per household. The only exception is for newlyweds. However, when the car loans are paid in full, newlyweds should follow the same rule. You want to allow room in your budget in case there is a reduction in income.

Besides loved ones, you want to make sure that unscrupulous people are not taking advantage of your good name by stealing your identity. Check your credit report every year to make sure the accounts on the report are accurate. If you do not agree with the information dispute it. You can dispute a charge either on the web or by phone. Once disputed the creditor is contacted to correct the information.

Lenders manage their credit wisely.

Credit Bureau Info

Transunion   www.transunion.com

Equifax   www.equifax.com

Experian   www.experian.com

Free Credit Report

www.annualcreditreport.com

Emotional Check Point

In chapters 2-5, there were a lot of instructions given. It is at this point where I have discovered that people check out of the process. Why? This process requires discipline. It is an inconvenience. One person stated that it is frustrating because it puts limits on what you can do. On the other hand, maybe you are reviewing the numbers and realize how much of your resources have been wasted on things that did not add value to your life. You may feel guilty. If either one of these scenarios describes where you are, be encouraged. It is natural to have these responses. However, you must push pass these emotions to effectively implement the strategy. It will be an inconvenience for a while. The length of time will depend on the amount of debt and the extent that the strategy is implemented. In order to help you beyond this point, I want you to consider the things that you truly want out of this life. What do you want to do? Who do you want to be? What is really necessary to make you content with who you are? What is your vision for your life? Think about this and jot down your answers. Make sure that your answers are focused on the things that you have control over. Exclude material possessions and dig deeper. Some examples are own a business, do outreach, and travel the world. Once you see the big picture you will gain momentum to move forward. What is your level of commitment? Let's take it up a notch. You can do this so let's do it!

My Vision

6

Overcoming Bill Collectors

I like to call them bullies. After all, that's how they behave. They call your phone, ask for you by your first name, and demand you pay them what and when they want. While you and I may not like it, they are paid to do it. After reading this chapter you will have the knowledge to put bill collectors in their place for good.

First and foremost you have consumer protection laws on your side. These are rules every debt collector must follow. There are serious penalties when the rules are not followed. The guidelines are very specific when it comes to certain things. The collectors must be considerate of your time by calling during decent hours. That means your phone should not be ringing before the crack of dawn and late at night. You must be notified of who they are, who they are trying to collect for, and how much they are trying to collect. If they become pesky, you have the ability to send a letter via certified mail telling them to cease contact. **This action will not make the bill disappear.** You must pay the bill if you owe it. If you do not owe the bill, then you can send a letter disputing the charges and it is up to the creditor to provide proof of the debt. Every time you speak with a collector, take notes with the individual's name, identification number, the time called, and the details discussed. This information may be needed in the event the collector does not play by the rules. It also comes in handy if different collector calls regarding the same bill. There are times when creditors make mistakes. It is for this reason that you listen to see if you actually owe the bill or if it is a mistake.

The next thing that is important in dealing with collectors is managing your emotions. There goes that emotional intelligence stuff again! How the conversation goes will depend greatly on how you perceive the situation. The person on the other side of the phone is just a person. They hold no special powers. They are not going to come through the phone and attack you. You are going to control the conversation not the collector. If you are unable to make a payment, say you are unable to make a payment at this time. If and when the person on the other end of the phone starts to belittle you, hang up the phone. If the person raises their voice at you, hang up the phone. At NO time do you allow anyone to make you feel worse about your situation. During the call, you are not to give any reasons why you cannot pay your bill. That is not their concern. Ask the collector the amount in which they will settle the account. This means you will pay less than what is actually owed. Once the amount is given, ask if that is the best that they can offer. You also want to know if it will be accepted as a onetime payment or installments. After paying the bill, request a letter showing that the account was settled and no other payments are needed. When you are able to make payments, it is my recommendation that you do it by mail. Personally, I am not fond of giving payment information over the phone. Do not agree to terms you cannot meet. Remember, your priorities are the things you need to survive. If the collector threatens to put it on your credit report, don't get alarmed. In most cases, it is true that the debt will have a negative impact on your credit report. The good news is you can recover from it. It is not the end of the world. It is a new beginning and sometimes in the game of life we have to press the reset button. Whenever you feel that you are at your breaking point, remember that you can and will survive this.

Lenders know they are the head and not the tail.

7

Everyday Financial Management

Every day we make decisions that will impact us in some way in the future. Our daily lives are made up of many choices (decisions). You may have chosen not to eat breakfast this morning. That choice resulted in a loud grumbling at 10 o'clock that you hoped no one else heard. Every day you make a choice regarding your finances. You decided not to pack your lunch so now you will either take someone's food from the office refrigerator or run through the closest drive-thru. It is the daily financial decisions that create a cascading effect for the days, weeks, months, and years to come. In this chapter you will find guidance to navigate through the everyday choices that impact your financial stability. Let's begin.

Keep a checkbook register

The age of online banking has brought upon the notion that a checkbook register is no longer required. After all, you can pick up your smart phone and check your available bank balance in no time flat. It rarely occurs to people that the numbers shown may not be correct. There are times when there are outstanding transactions that do not appear on the register.

A checkbook register is your financial GPS. It tells you where you are going, how long it will take to get there, how many miles you have to the next pit stop (payday), and whether you will need to take a detour (unexpected bills).

Would you go on a road trip without a navigation system? No? Well do not go forward on your financial journey without a checkbook register.

Limit Your Swipes

The debit card has replaced cash for most of us. Who carries cash anymore? You do not need to carry cash because just about everywhere you go accepts debit cards. Cash helped limit spending because as the cash decreased, there was a visualization of the amount of money getting smaller and smaller. When using a debit card, the visualization is not there. It is not until you check the bank register or balance your check register that you realize that you have over spent. It is for this reason you should limit your swipes. If you are going shopping, designate the amount of money you plan to spend and limit your swipes to that amount. Carrying cash may be the best solution for you if you struggle in this area.

Avoid Unnecessary Fees

Late fees and over the limit fees are premiums paid to companies that you can be doing something else with. Think of it this way. Your cellular phone provider charges ten dollars a month as a late fee. Over a year's time that is $120 a year. Your bank is so nice to process the transactions that your account does not have enough money to cover (overdrafts). As a token of its generosity, the bank only charges $35 or more for this courtesy. In order to be financially successful you must avoid giving your money away to cover fees.

Dump That Pay Card

Pay cards have been seen as the answer for those who do not have bank accounts. As a financially educated individual, you realize that paying someone else to access the money you have worked so hard for is not a wise decision. You understand the importance of having a bank account rather than a pay card. If your employer requires you to have direct deposit, open a bank account. Steer clear of pay cards period.

Examine You Check Stub

One day I was talking to a couple of friends and they said that they never check their check stubs. I immediately exclaimed 'What kind of foolishness is that!' That is putting a lot of trust in the people who process your paycheck. As humans, we make mistakes. It is up to you to watch your money and make sure that the human processing you payroll check did not make an error and short you 2 hours. You cannot trust that others will take care of your money without you verifying that they are doing what they are supposed to do. Always, always, always check you paycheck stub.

Don't Try To Cheat Uncle Sam

Simply stated, pay your taxes. It's amazing to me how many people are in financial trouble because they were trying to be clever and cheat the IRS. Those are three letters I personally do not play with. If you are not exempt from taxes, do not put exempt on your W-4 form. How do you know whether or not you are exempt? If you had to send the IRS a check last year to pay taxes, you are not exempt. Go to human resources and correct your W-4. Yes, this will decrease the amount of take home pay you will have but you will not have the burden of the IRS on your back.

Review you income tax return carefully. Make sure that the dependents are correct. Verify that the credits that are shown on the form are the ones you are eligible for and can be proven in the event you are audited. If you do not understand something ask the person that is doing your taxes to explain it. Ultimately, if there is something wrong and you got more money than you should have gotten, you will have to pay it back with interest. Long story short, pay your taxes.

Plan Ahead

One of the essential factors to financial stability is planning. Planning helps make life easier. While you certainly cannot plan for everything that can happen, you can be prepared for the everyday. When getting fiscally fit, I often prescribe that the amount spent for lunch is reduced. This means take a sack lunch. In order to be successful with this, you must plan what you will have for lunch ahead of time. Plan where you money is going to go. The budget will play a major role in the planning process. If you are planning a vacation, determine how much you will have to save in order to have the trip paid for before you go. The next chapter will tell you more about saving.

Share Expenses

At the very beginning of the book I shared that individuals who were on Social Security were able to live fulfilling lives. At the time of this book, the minimum Social Security allotment is $721 a month. One secret to their success is sharing expenses. A responsible roommate can make your financial life much easier. A roommate provides the benefit of opening up more money to get out of debt or build a nice size nest egg. Be sure to check out the potential roommate's credit history. You want to make sure that you are not stuck with bills.

I would hate for you to have to go on one of those judge shows to get your money back.

Lenders practice financial management every day.

8

It's Time to SAVE

Growing up I spent a lot of time with a couple of cousins. We were right around the same ages. These cousins had piggy banks all around their rooms with money in all of them. I had a pink bank shaped like a little girl that stood about two and a half feet tall. My piggy bank never got close to being half full. Needless to say, I did not understand why they saved their money when there were so many things to buy like penny cookies, bubble gum, and candy cigarettes. They would say that they were saving their money for a rainy day.

I thought that made absolutely no sense. What did a rainy day have to do with saving money? When I became an adult I realized what it meant to save for a rainy day.

The art of saving is another thing that plays a major role in your financial health. It is a practice that is often passed down to children from their parents. Since saving was not a lesson taught to me as a child, I found it challenging to implement as an adult. Never the less, I overcame the challenge and so will you.

All the financial gurus have different names for savings accounts. In this book it will be referred to as a **contingency fund**. One thing my cousins knew that I didn't was the rainy day is going to come. How well you weather the rainy day will depend greatly on how well you are prepared. You do not want to get caught in the rain without an umbrella because you will get drenched. It would be nice to have a raincoat and some goulashes along with the umbrella. The contingency fund, not a credit card, is your rainy day outfit. This is where you save money for the unexpected expenses and the nonrecurring bills. Examples of what to save for in this fund include home repairs, automobile repairs, vacations, unemployment, sickness and emergencies. It can also be used to build up a nest egg for an initial investment account. If you are trying to accumulate money in one place for a particular occasion, place it in the contingency fund. The fund should not be mixed with you bill paying account. Place the fund in a central location whether it is a savings account at the bank, a mattress, or a jar under the dog house.

Many employers offer other saving accounts that are useful. A Christmas Club account allows you to save money for the holidays and earn interest. A Health Savings Account (HSA) allows money to be saved for health related expenses. The HSA has a tax benefit. There are retirement savings accounts such as 401K and 403B. These are great to have but they do not replace the contingency fund. These accounts should be in addition to the contingency fund.

There are a number of suggestions on how much money to save for emergencies. The economy and job market will play a critical role in the amount that is needed. The main idea is to start saving something. It must be consistent. Every month you must put something in the contingency fund. Place your best gift, to you, that is affordable in the fund. This may mean cutting an expense that was discussed in chapter four. For the sake of clarity, putting money in the contingency fund is a must. This is a budget item. It should appear after the necessities and before the luxuries. It does not matter if it is five dollars a pay period. Put something in the fund.

There are so many benefits to the contingency fund. Here are a few things to expect as the fund grows.

- Greater self esteem
- Less restrictions
- Less expenses
- Greater security
- Less worry about finances

I want to encourage those who have children in your lives to impart the wisdom of saving. It will have a tremendous impact on their financial lives when they become adults. It may be the difference between prosperity and poverty.

Protect Your Savings

As your savings begin to grow, others will notice the new confidence you will have regarding your finances. You will be seen by others as a person with means. You will be seen as someone who can spare a few dollars. When this shift occurs you will start receiving all sorts of requests. These requests will include lending money, investing in some type of business, or someone selling a product. The requests will come from both people who are close to you and those not so close to you. It is ultimately your decision whether or not to honor these requests by dipping into your contingency fund. Please consider these things before withdrawing money from the fund. If the request is to borrow money, will you receive this money back? A rule of thumb I use is if I can't afford to give the money away then I can't afford to lend it. Also, ask yourself if the person spends their money wisely. If the answer is no, you may want to reconsider allowing them to borrow money. If someone approaches you to invest in a business, treat him/her in the same way that a bank would treat him/her. Request a copy of the business plan and ask how much money s/he is investing in the business. If this cannot be provided, respectfully decline the request to invest. By the way, investing means you will get your money back plus interest. If the request is for you to buy something, consider whether or not the item is something you really need. If the item is something that will add another bill to your budget you want to avoid buying it.

Lenders SAVE!

9

Become a Giver

Something strange happens when people accumulate money. Some people realize that they can have an impact on others by sharing. Some people become so in love with their money that they hold on to every penny. Others let their desire to be better than others take hold and start showing off their money. Greed is a terrible emotional state that I have personally seen ruin many lives. Greedy individuals can turn into hustlers that manipulate to accumulate more. It really does not matter how much is acquired, it is never enough. This behavior turns the individuals into people that others do not trust. As greed manifests itself, the empire that was created will crumble. The only thing that combats greed is generosity. There are universal laws that have been proven to be true for many centuries. The law of reciprocity is one. The law of reciprocity is as one gives one will receive. In order to receive one must give.

Maybe at this time you do not have the funds to give money. If this is the case, give your time and your talents. You can give to charity, church, and individuals. As long as you are a giver you reduce the possibility that greed will take over your life.

Being generous also is smart when it comes to paying taxes back to Uncle Sam. Have you ever wondered why businesses give money to charity? Part of the reason is the businesses want to be considered good corporate citizens. They want the community to believe that their presence has a positive impact. The other reason they give to charity is it reduces the tax burden. Wouldn't you like to decide where your money goes? If you are paying Uncle Sam back annually, amp up your contributions to reduce your tax burden. Your church or other charity will make good use of your contribution.

Special Note: The tax benefit applies when itemized deductions exceed the standard deduction. Please consult a tax professional for more in-depth information.

Lenders know how to share.

10

Couples & Money

Money is one of the three things that cause divorce. Since this is a book on being fiscally fit, it is only befitting that money and relationships should be addressed. Things have changed a lot since the women's movement. More and more women are in the workforce. The economic demands in many communities require two incomes to live comfortable. When you are dating, you have the opportunity to find out all kinds of things about your partner. The thing that is often overlooked is how your potential mate manages his/her finances. That's the last thing on your mind. You are focused on those good looks and that wonderful smile. It is at the point that the couple becomes engaged that finances should be discussed.

When you become engaged, you need to reveal to your fiancé all outstanding debt. You should be completely honest about who you owe. If you are living paycheck to paycheck, only because you have not started applying the information in this book, let your partner know. The reaction you receive may not be what you hoped for, but if the person is really committed to you the person will still marry you. Do this well before the wedding day.

Well, you are already married and it is too late to discuss your student loans and credit card debt. Above anything else you need to decide and decree that money issues will not destroy your marriage. Once you have made this decision you can move forward. You and your spouse will need to set up a time where you can discuss you finances. Decide whether one is better than the other with the finances. If you know deep down that you suck in this area, let go of your pride and let the other person manage the finances. This does not mean that you are not an active part of how the finances are spent. Both of you will follow the budget that was discussed in chapter three. Both of you will be accountable to each other. Each couple should have a joint checking and savings account. The checking account is the account in which the bills will be paid. The joint savings account is the account that the couple saves money for the couple. You may find it necessary to have a personal bank account as well. There is nothing wrong with this. It is encouraged especially in cases when one of the individuals is a spender. Each couple has something that works for them. Find what works for you and use it.

Reduce expenses as much as possible. When you first marry you both may have car payments. Outside of this period, there should only be one car payment at a time. Qualify for your home mortgage based on only one of your incomes. Ideally, your expenses should be low enough that if one of you were to get sick or laid-off, the other would be able to cover all the expenses. The most important thing is to work together. Read this book together. If you have trouble getting started, call a financial coach to help you. During this process, remember that this is not a time of pointing fingers, name calling, or punching below the belt. That will get you nowhere. Work together and respect each other. Define your financial goals and use the information in the book to help you reach them. As mentioned before, this process will not be complete overnight. It takes a while to change habits. It could take a year or it could take five years. Both of you must be committed to the process. Besides, you have until death do you part to get it right.

Lenders take time to get their financial affairs in order at home.

What's next?

You will see your finances take shape. You will have money in the bank and no credit card debt. You will be feeling good. You may even start helping others get on track. At this point you are ready to learn more about finances. Continue to read to learn more. Subscribe to magazines that focus on money management. It may all seem like a foreign language at first, but you will start to piece it together.

I wish you much financial success. You are now well on your way to being the lender.

Live Well & Prosper

L. Gray

www.ingramcontent.com/pod-product-compliance
Lightning Source LLC
Chambersburg PA
CBHW071758170526
45167CB00003B/1082